# The Ultimate Money-Saving Merchant Account Rescue System

## CLARK PIERSON

# DEDICATION

This book is for every business in the United States who accepts credit cards grudgingly (rightfully so). It's for those who are fed up with wildly expensive credit card processing fees. Fed up with ridiculously absurd contracts and cancellation charges. For those who have spent and continue to spend countless hours frustratingly on hold with impossible to understand, thick accented and outsourced customer service centers. I hope this book helps you overcome every one of these challenges and much more besides.

# CONTENTS

# INTRODUCTION

This book is not meant to be read cover to cover for enjoyment purposes. It is meant to be a reference guide to arm yourself with when shopping, reviewing or re-negotiating your merchant account so you don't get taken advantage of.

It is meant to show you the proper way to go about getting a great deal, and avoid shockingly expensive pit-falls, so your business can "live long and prosper." There are many pit-falls, scams and rip-off practices unfortunately to look out for. I will help you execute a NO B.S approach that is time tested.

# IS THE COSTS TO ACCEPT CREDIT CARDS REALLY WORTH IT?

In this chapter, we're going to discuss the actual credit card transaction process. We'll talk about the real costs and risks for banks, processors and merchants to run credit card transactions.

Having this basic knowledge of the bankcard process will give you some perspective as to why you are charged the way you are to accept electronic transactions in your business.

Just know that NOBODY likes to pay these rates and fees to accept payments. After reading this chapter however, I think you will come to realize that the costs associated with accepting credit cards is an unbelievable deal for the business owner.

If you don't feel that way at the moment, don't worry.

You are like 98% of the people reading this book. Trust me, I get it.

### Why would I want to pay these processing costs?

I understand the huge frustration lots of business owners experience, when they take at glance at their monthly credit card processing statement and see substantial fees taken out for accepting that form of payment.

This inevitably causes them to wonder, "If I wasn't accepting credit cards and didn't have to pay those mandatory fees, I would have so much more take - home pay that I could put towards advertising, expanding or even giving myself a well-deserved pay increase."

But here's the reality. Like I mentioned at the beginning of this chapter, it is actually a great deal for merchants to accept credit cards. Despite your previous experiences with your merchant account, it's not a hindrance whatsoever, it's a revenue driving tool.

Let me tell you why I believe this. It is actually statistically proven that customers who purchase a product at your place of business will pay up to 35% more with a credit card then they ever would with cash or check.

This is a fact of life worth taking note of for the small business owner. So I will repeat it. A customer will spend up to 35% more to purchase a product with a credit card, than they EVER would by way of cash or check. 35% more! This is an undeniable reality of today's consumer.

Unless you are getting charged 35% to accept each credit card transaction, I would say your business is blessed to accept 35% additional revenue generated just by accepting all forms of payments.

Later in this chapter I'm going to talk about the actual costs and risks associated with taking a credit card. However not for the business owner, but for every other party involved in the transaction process. The business owner actually has the sweetest deal out of everyone involved in the transaction and I'll tell you why momentarily.

Some other obvious benefits of accepting credit card besides more revenue (which I shamelessly believe is its most important feature) is it's easy to track and manage all of your transactions. Because merchant accounts are electronic, there's an obvious digital record of all transaction data, which makes life easier for you to keep an accounting of your business.

It can save you serious time versus having to add everything up on a regular basis (also account for human error problem solving sessions) and bank trips to deposit cash and checks. Because merchant accounts have such detailed reporting of all transaction data, it inevitably avoids potential theft from employees in your business. This would not initially seem like such a big deal that is until it has happened to you. Then it's a merchant account's most coveted feature.

# What are the steps in a credit card transaction?

THE PROCESS

Step 1: An individual finds a bank that will issue a credit card for them to use. This bank is called the issuing bank because it issues the credit card to the person who pays the bill at the end of the day. This individual (now called the cardholder) must have the creditworthiness to receive a card because the issuing bank will be the one who takes the risk by providing the funds up front, on the cardholder's behalf. In doing so, the issuing bank is providing the funds in the form of credit.

Step 2: Front-End. The cardholder goes to a retailer, a dealer, a vendor, a restaurant or anyone else who accepts credit cards. These establishments are called merchants. The customer purchases a product or service from a merchant, swiping their credit card through a machine called a credit card terminal (also known as transaction equipment). In many restaurants and other companies using a software program, there is a small magnetic stripe reader attached to the merchant's computer that is used in place of a terminal.

NOTE: In order to accept cards, the merchant has to set up a relationship with an acquiring bank. An acquiring bank is a bank that will receive (acquire) the funds at the end of the transaction process and place it into the merchant's account. One bank pays the funds for the cardholder (the issuing bank); the other receives the funds on behalf of the merchant (the acquiring bank).

Step 3: When the card is swiped, the information on the credit card is read by the terminal and is sent to the merchant's acquiring bank. The terminal sends out this information to ask the issuing bank if the credit card is open and has funds available for the purchase. This is called a sales authorization request. In effect, the terminal is asking, "I am requesting that you authorize the validity and acceptability of this card. Will you authorize me to accept it or not?"

Step 4: The acquiring bank sends the information to a processor. The purpose of the processor is to determine what kind of credit card is coming through and where it is to route the transaction. If it is Visa, then it routes the transaction information through the Visa network; if it is MasterCard then it sends the information through the MasterCard system, and so on. Visa, MasterCard and other credit card companies are known in the industry as associations.

Step 5: The processor routes the transaction to the association.

Step 6: Once the association receives the transaction information, it routes the information to the cardholder's issuing bank. There are many issuing banks to service so many cardholders.

Step 7: The issuing bank checks its records to ensure that the credit card has not been reported stolen, has not gone over its limit, and so on. The issuing bank has the final say as to whether the credit card transaction is approved or declined. For this example, we'll say that the credit card transaction meets the approval of the issuing bank.

Step 8: The issuing bank sends back to the association an approval code, also known as an authorization code.

Step 9: The association receives this information and sends the authorization code back to the processing company (processor).

Step 10: Once the processor receives the response from the association, it routes the information back to the merchant's acquiring bank.

Step 11: The acquiring bank then routes the authorization code back to the merchant's terminal that sent out the transaction in the first place.

Step 12: Once the merchant's terminal receives the information from the acquiring bank, the terminal prints out a receipt with the approval or authorization code, and the merchant is then required to get the cardholder to sign the receipt to confirm that the transaction took place. Once signed, the cardholder will be obligated to pay the issuing bank for the amount approved.

Steps 2 through 12 occur in only 3-5 seconds!

Step 13: Back-End. At the end of the day, the merchant has one more step. The acquiring bank does not know if the transaction was signed. The merchant is required to fully complete this transaction by letting the acquiring bank know that all of the transactions during the day were signed. After reviewing all of their sales, returns, and voided transactions, the merchant finalizes the sales by sending the completed transactions to the acquiring bank. This procedure is known as closing or batching out. If this step is not done, the merchant will not receive their money. Closing or batching out is something that can occur automatically or can be done manually. This is up to the merchant. Ordinarily, batching out is done manually when there is a restaurant or a service providing tips. Think how it works when you go to a restaurant: You give the waiter your credit card. They swipe the card with the amount of the food but this transaction is done before you leave a tip. Sometime after you leave the restaurant, the waiter receives your signed receipt with a tip added on to it. Frequently, waiters and waitresses do not have time to input tips into the transaction equipment until the end of the day. Once the tips are entered into the terminal, then the actual amount charged (food charge plus tip) is completed and the information is stored in the terminal. Batching is the process of sending the finalized transactions from the terminal to the acquiring bank.

Step 14: Once the transaction information is sent by the terminal to the acquiring bank, a process called settlement begins. The acquiring bank receives the batch information directly from the merchant's terminal. The merchant wants the acquiring bank to deposit the appropriate funds into its bank account. But it's not that simple; there are also fees associated with every credit card transaction. They are known in the industry as discount fees and transaction fees.

Step 15: When the acquiring bank gets the settlement or batch information from the merchant's terminal, it routes this information back to the processing company and the steps toward settlement (transferring all of the funds and fees to the appropriate companies) begin. It is not necessary at this point to know what happens step-by-step on the settlement side. What is important to know is that the acquiring bank ultimately receives the funds, but only after discount fees and per item fees have been calculated and deducted, and deposits the net amount into the merchant's bank account. For example, the merchant might have batched out an amount of $1,000. After determining what fees are to be paid to the association, the processing company and to the banks, maybe only $970 is deposited into the merchant's account. It usually takes 24-48 hours for the funds to be transferred into the merchant's account.

Step 16: The issuing bank sends a monthly billing statement to the cardholder.

Step 17: The cardholder pays his issuing bank. Still with me? Good.

Bet you didn't think the process could be so complicated right?

### What is the risk involved for taking a credit card?

Like I said earlier, accepting credit cards is a great deal for business owners. There is however substantial risk for banks who issue credit cards to your customers. And they have to protect themselves against this real risk by way of transaction fees passed onto you. At first this seems unfair that business owners are taking on the burden of the risk that banks face by issuing credit cards. Let me explain the way it works.

Let's say a customer comes into your store and purchases a $100 item, and they choose to purchase it using a credit card. In the bank's reality what happens is, the bank floats that customer a small loan essentially. Because the customer chose to pay with a credit card instead of using cash or writing a check which requires the money to be in the customer's checking account, it is an actual small loan the bank is giving to that customer.

Now the business owner is guaranteed that $100 no matter what, once a transaction is settled. There is no risk whatsoever of not getting the $100. A customer could max out his credit card at your store, with a small bank loan by way of an issued credit card, and the business will see that money at the end of the day whether the customer pays the bank back or not.

The bank usually gives the customer about 45 days to repay them without any penalty. The truth to understand clearly is that customers don't always pay the bank back. That is a fact of life and a big risk that banks who issue credit cards take on.

Banks often times have to eat the unpaid costs of what they loaned a customer, because they may not get it back at the end of the day. Because there's that element of risks involved, and banks can't afford just to give millions of small loans with no repayment, they have a small transaction fee that comes out of your credit card processing account on each transaction. A good portion of that transaction fee covers the cost of losses for the bank when a customer decides not to pay its loan back.

Like I said earlier and will continue to preach, business owners are getting a steal of a deal, because they get that bank loaned money no matter what at the end of the day. Additionally they pay a small transaction fee to accept a form of payment that delivers up to 35% more revenue spent on the exact same products and services in their businesses. In my book that is a good deal.

However, if you still feel like your rates and fees to accept cards are to heavy to bare, chances are, they might be. I'll discussed later how to determine if you are paying to much.

**Out of those involved in the transaction process, who keeps the majority of the rates and fees that business owners have to pay?**

When I explained what takes place in a credit card transaction you were introduced to the players involved to make that transaction possible. Because there is cost associated when each player involves themselves in the transaction process, each player is entitled to a portion of the merchant account fees that is required to run a transaction. I am not going to go over the split that each player receives per transaction, however I will discuss the more important ones as it relates to a business owner.

We just discussed the risk that falls on banks who issue credit cards to consumers. Because card issuing banks take on such a hefty amount of risk, it seems perfectly logical that they're entitled to the biggest portion of the transaction fees that are assessed to the business for accepting electronic payments.

Additionally, the credit card processing company that you have a merchant account through receives a portion of the rates and fees, for servicing your account, providing equipment, ongoing customer service, and the accounting involved in preparing a statement at the end of the month.

And last but not least, a decent portion of the rates and fees go to the card association's Visa, MasterCard, Discover, and American Express for allowing access to their network to process cards.

## What if my business just stopped accepting credit cards?

I wouldn't be in the business I'm currently in if I thought that the best answer to manageable credit card processing costs, was for the business owner to just cancel their merchant account altogether.

To be blunt this is not an intelligent strategy for a number of different reasons. First off, this method will result in less revenue for your business. The fact is that more and more people are demanding to pay electronically for everything they purchase.

The driving force behind this demand is psychological in nature. They demand to pay electronically because it's more painful psychologically to pay with cash or check, than it is to pay with a credit or debit card.

For instance, let's say you have a large pile of money in your hand when you walk into the grocery store to do your weekly shopping. You choose to use cash to pay for the grocery bill at the checkout counter. As you're handing over that cash, the once large pile of money you walked in with starts to dwindle in your hand. Psychologically there is actual pain associated with this process.

On the other hand when you choose to pay by credit card, there's no dwindling pile of cash in your hand to feel pain over. You can simply swipe with no immediate remorse. At checkout, it's an unemotional process for the customer. And that's why they'll pay and swipe up to 35% more per transaction on any given item than they ever would with cash and check.

The other big reason I advocate against canceling your merchant account, is from a customer satisfaction point of view. Like I said earlier, people are demanding to pay by credit card. It's the way of the present and surely the future.

Customers are at the moment paying with credit cards that are embedded into their cell phones. At the end of the day, if your product or service is a commodity, and you choose not to accept credit cards, customers will simply walk down the street to your closest competitor who does accept credit cards.

## Why is it so confusing to understand credit card processing?

This is really a very understandable question and I get it a lot from frustrated merchants. First off, just accept that it's a confusing process. Your frustration with its complexity won't change a thing.

This is one reason it is really, really important that you have a good agent that you are comfortable with and can trust, who can explain everything to you in a way that you can understand before you jump into a merchant account.

We'll talk about an agent's real value a little later, but if you don't thoroughly understand the terms, conditions and pricing of your merchant account agreement, than your agent and YOU have failed and run the risk of having your account riddled with hidden fees.

One of the reasons it's very confusing is because there are many players involved in the actual transaction process. You got Visa, MasterCard, Discover, American Express, an ISO (Independent Sales Organization), Processor, member bank, and an acquiring bank. A lot of separate entities all working together to make a credit card transaction happen in under a few seconds for your business.

Because of the complex nature of the process, and all of the separate entities involved to make things work, the monthly statements you receive each month are a true reflection of its complexity.

All involved entities have to get paid for the associated risk they take on one way or another, and there's really no simple way to reflect it ETHICALLY on your statement without making it confusing.

Again, embrace the complexity. The entities are not being confusing just for the heck of it. This doesn't excuse you from learning it despite its complexity however. Never wise to enter into any type agreement without first thoroughly understanding how you are charged.

### Wrapping it up.

My hope for this chapter is that even though you may be upset (rightly so) with the credit card processing industry as a whole, you realize that business owners get a good deal that gives them more revenue versus just accepting cash or check, and satisfies their customer's wishes for electronic transaction acceptance.

I understand that this knowledge accomplishes very little if you are in a situation where you have been taken advantage of through wildly expensive or even hidden processing rates and fees.

That's why we will be discussing rates in the next chapter.

# HOW DO I GET THE BEST RATES?

In this chapter, I'm going to be talking about all things in regards to your credit card processing rate. When you swipe a credit card, there's a monetary rate or percentage associated with swiping that card. This is probably not news to you.

We all unfortunately know that credit card processing salesmen call and walk into your business unannounced anywhere from three to five times a day (depending on where you do business) always claiming to beat your current rate.

This chapter will give you clarity as to what they're talking about, and if they're trying to manipulate you in any type of way with regards to your rates.

# What are the different pricing structures?

You might wonder who establishes these rates, fees, and charges. Why do they exist and why have they been set up the way they are? I will answer these questions and help familiarize you with the various credit and debit card charges and what each one represents. By gaining an understanding of this section, you will be far ahead in your knowledge of pricing than sadly many merchant service agents. How great will that be for you though!

Interchange is a series of combined fees that occurs when a credit or debit card transaction takes place. The main reason for Interchange is to compensate the issuing banks for the risk they take in providing the funds to the merchant on behalf of the cardholder. The risk taken by the issuing banks is two-fold: (1) The cardholder has use of the bank's money for as much as 45 days, interest free, before they have to pay the bill. The issuing banks providing these funds are not guaranteed they will be repaid for the credit card transaction by the cardholder. (2) There is a risk that the card might be stolen and/or used fraudulently, and the issuing bank risks losses incurred by providing the merchant the funds before discovering the bad news. To cover these losses, and to make a profit as well, a fee has been established by the issuing banks and the acquiring banks, working together with Visa, MasterCard, and other association members. This group was formed as a cooperative. The cooperative was developed to create a system of charges (Interchange) that would be uniform throughout the merchant services industry and guarantee the transfer of funds from bank to bank throughout the country and eventually throughout the world.

The system of interchange fees consists of three parts: (1) a rate, (2) a per-item fee; and (3) an assessment fee. These charges change frequently.

**Rate (Discount Fee or Discount Rate)**

In every credit card transaction, a percentage of the money received from the purchase is deducted from the merchant. The purpose of this fee is to pay the issuing bank. This fee, known as the discount rate, is deducted from the merchant during settlement, so when the merchant receives their money, the fee is discounted from the full amount. For example, a cardholder purchases an item from a merchant for $100.00. Let's say the rate is 1.54%. When the $100 is transferred from the issuing bank, a fee of $1.54 is given back to the issuing bank before sending the balance to the merchant.

Discount rates are based on risk. The higher the risk, the higher the rate. For instance, if this $100 transaction was manually entered into the terminal because the machine could not read the credit card, the transaction would qualify as a mid- qualified transaction. This higher risk – going from a qualified transaction to a mid- qualified transaction – is known as a downgrade. Downgrades are more expensive, because the quality and risk of the transaction is downgraded from the highest-quality and lowest risk-transaction, or qualified transaction. The increased risk and lower quality change the category of this transaction from a tier-one transaction (qualified) to a tier-two transaction (mid-qualified). The rate (the percentage charged) increases from, e.g., 1.54% to 1.85%. Thus, instead of a fee of $1.54 being charged to the merchant for the $100 transaction example above, the higher-risk transaction increases the fee from the issuing bank to $1.85. Now let's say the merchant accepts the $100 charge as an order over the telephone. The risk increases even more. The discount rate is increased to an even higher amount than the tier-two rate. This card-not-present transaction falls into the tier-three transaction category - a non-qualified transaction. Let's say the non-qualified rate is 2.99%. The merchant would now be charged $2.99 on the $100 credit card transaction to pay the issuing bank instead of the original $1.54 that took place when the transaction was a qualified rate.

**Per-Item Fee**

On each transaction, there is an additional charge called the per-item fee. Why is there another fee when the discount fee already exists? In some transactions, the credit card is declined and there is no authorization code sent. This means no funds transfer will take place, but the issuing bank has still had to check the card. The computer systems in place to pass this information back and forth create a considerable expense. To defray the cost of the transaction process, there is a per- item fee. Unlike the discount rate, the per-item fee for all three tiers could be the same. The most common charge for per-item fees, as of today's Interchange rates, is ten cents per transaction. In the example above, using the qualified rate, the merchant pays $1.54 plus $.10, or a total of $1.64 for the transaction.

**Assessment**

This is a standard fee used by Visa, MasterCard and Discover in all of their transactions, no matter which tier. This is the primary way that Visa, MasterCard and Discover make their money. Today, the assessment fee is .0950% for MasterCard and .0925% for Visa and Discover for virtually every transaction that takes place, whether a credit or a debit card is used. So, returning to our example above, the merchant accepts a Visa card, charging the cardholder $100. Because it is at a qualified rate, or a tier one transaction, the rate is 1.54%, plus the $.10 per-item fee, for a total of $1.64. Now Visa charges the assessment fee and adds it to the rate. The merchant pays $1.64 plus $.0925, or $1.7325 for the $100 transaction.

Besides the tiered pricing structure mentioned above there is another common way that merchants can be priced for taking credit cards. It's called interchange-plus pricing. Here is a simple way to think about this interchange-plus pricing model.

Interchange as explained above is the set of rates established by Visa, MasterCard, Discover...etc.

The word "plus" refers to the agent or processor's markup that is added to each transaction. The markup is usually expressed as "Basis Points."

Basis Points are equal to 1/100th of a percent or 0.01%. For example take Visa's current interchange fee for a swiped card of 1.54%. Measured in basis points, this fee would be one hundred and fifty four basis points (1.54% = 154 basis points).

Think of "Interchange" as the wholesale cost to process credit cards and the "Plus" as the retail markup for processors. No tier system when talking about this pricing structure. Every transaction is assessed the Interchange rate and then the basis points are added to it to end up with the final discount rate.

## What to be leery of when talking about rates.

It is brutally easy to get manipulated when talking about processing rates. As you now understand from the previous chapter, this process is confusing with lots of moving parts and complexity involved. Because of its complex nature, it has become common place to be okay with ignorance to its details. And with business owners in ignorance of how they are charged to accept cards, it has become common practice for sleazy processing salesman to scam businesses every which way unfortunately. This is a major reason many merchants nationwide are displeased with the merchant services industry and the way they explain and present rates.

Often times, when a salesman walks into your business and offers to lower your rate, what they're talking about is your *"Effective Rate."* You actually pay hundreds of different rates, because Visa, MasterCard, Discover, and American Express assign a different rate for each type of card, and the way the card is taken by the business owner.

That's why we talked about tiered pricing structures. Each one of those cards fits into a specified tier, or you have processing companies that add a slight markup to the wholesale cost to process the card. If you remember this is called interchange-plus pricing.

Here is how to correctly understand what an effective rate is. At the end of the month when all is said and done, if you divide the amount of transaction volume by the cost associated to take those transactions, you will get what's called the *"Effective Rate."* It's the one number assigned for that month. It could be different each month depending on the specific type of card you take and what tier it fits into.

The thing to be careful of when talking about your effective rate is being aware that it could be different every single month. Salesman who place a heavy emphasis on effective rate are typically trying to simplify the sales process because they aren't educated or experienced enough to know that they are doing damaged with this approach. Many are ignorant to the fact that it furthers the adversarial relationship between processors and merchants when the "promised" effective rate changes on a month to month basis.

So, rather than entertaining a heavy discussion on effective rate from a door to door salesman, shift the conversation to what they can do for you depending on if you are on a tiered pricing structure, or interchange plus pricing. You need to be aware of what pricing structure you're on, in order to effectively negotiate your pricing. Otherwise it's like throwing darts in the dark. You may get lucky and hit the bulls-eye, but chances are, it's a long drawn out process of trial and error.

If you have an honest and educated agent you're working with, he can determine your structure, no problem. Don't ever let a salesman try to pitch you an effective rate under the guise that you only have one rate you pay for every single transaction that your business generates. It's just not true.

Additionally it's very easy for salesman to manipulate you by emphasizing a low swiped rate, but then raising the keyed in rate where the majority of your transactions fall into on the back-end. Be aware of the entire merchant account proposal. Never just a single rate. There are definitely other considerations to think about, versus just a good rate.

## How do I know if I have good rates?

Most business owners would determine a good rate to be the cheapest rate, and in my experience that's just not the case. When you shop merchant accounts with only a cheap price in mind, you can expect lots of headaches, very, very poor service, and typically a crappy piece of equipment. And sadly usually some hidden or made up fees on the back end. This is shockingly common. Credit card processors are not going to pay out so you can accept credit cards. You are smart. You are a business owner. Can you sell products below your cost and stay afloat? No. It doesn't work like that. Be skeptical if the pricing looks to good to be true, because it just might be.

So again, I would recommend that some suspicion be raised if your rates are too cheap because your agent and processor is not going to work for free - nor should they work for free. They need to get paid in the transaction process as well for the work that is being done on their end.  If your rates are way too low per transaction, you'll never see your agent again after they set you up. Not to get off topic here but I want you to think about something really quick. When was the last time you saw or spoke to the person that set up your merchant account? Month, 6 months, 2 years...etc? If you have gone longer than 6 months this may be an indicator to you that your account is not worth his time because you are priced to low, and your account may have some hidden fees to make up for your seemingly low rate. Good time to find a new agent typically. Anyway, back to what we were discussing earlier.

To give you a rough pricing baseline to determine if you are in an appropriate range, make sure your rates fall within the .89 % to 3.5%  rate range.

Also realize that pricing is specifically set to cover the risk of the business. That's why there is an underwriting process when setting up a merchant account, just like an insurance policy. There is risk of non-payment from the cardholder to the bank. So in the underwriting process when a processor is determining what rate is acceptable, you will have to answer questions like

1. How long have you been in business?

2. Have you ever had a processor terminate your merchant account?

3. Do you have any open or prior bankruptcies?

Not every business is entitled to the same rate structure and pricing because the risk factor is not the same all across the board. You will have to work closely with an agent that you know, like and trust who can assure you that you're on the right pricing structure, with the right rates, for your specific type of business.

### Are there other factors consider besides a good rate?

There are TONS of other factors to consider besides just a low rate. Most merchants get manipulated on rate because they are so focused on it from the get-go. And it makes sense why they are so focused on it. Every single credit card processing salesman who walks into their business attempting to win their merchant account, all talk about the exact same thing. Lower rates, lower rates, lower rates...

So when a business owner decides to actually shop their merchant account, literally the only thing on their mind is, "I have to get a good rate." Because it is drilled into their head 3-5 times per work day, of course that is what they are going to consider the most important or only factor.

Rarely are business owners concerned or even aware of their actual monthly fees, as they are about their rates. You see, you have your rate structure which always involves a pretty heavy discussion, and then you have your monthly fees which usually are never talked about. Monthly fees are typically a flat fee versus a percentage. So unlike a rate or percentage you pay that is based off of your transaction volume, your monthly fees are assessed whether you process $1,000,000 or $0. You will be assessed your monthly fees regardless of volume. Usually when a business owner realizes this, they suddenly would like to talk about their monthly fees and not just their assigned processing rates.

It is important to note that in the assigned monthly fees that merchants are charged, I find more made up and hidden charges than anywhere else within a merchant account. Because of its somewhat unregulated nature, the processing industry can easily make up their own monthly fees and tack it on whenever they want. So here is a common scenario:

*You sign up with a credit card processing company because they promise you the most competitive rates you have ever seen. You have many friends who own businesses and they all pay way more than this processing company is promising to charge you (red flag!). Years go by until you notice that you haven't seen or heard from your agent or processing company since you were initially setup (red flag!). A friend gets into the merchant services industry and wants to practice giving you a quote, so you give him your monthly statement to look at and warn him that you have unbeatable rates. He comes back with a proposal regardless and admits your rates are good. However, he points out all the monthly fees you have been paying for years without your knowledge. You don't remember discussing these monthly fees when you were setup? Most likely because they were never discussed. Your friend even admits that he has no idea what some of these fees are. Usually those are the ones that are made up to cover for the low rates that you were promised. You call your processing company and have a nightmare of a time locating your agent. Everyone you speak with is justifying their actions with industry specific jargon and you have no idea what they are talking about. Worst of all, and fed up with your processor and agent, you attempt to cancel and they drop the bomb that you are in a long term contract with a HUGE cancellation fee to get out.*

I have seen this exact story and hundreds like it unfortunately and its high frequency occurrence is sickening.

There are many fees that can be added to or taken away from your merchant account at any given time, and you need to be aware of them as a business owner. They can be substantial. We'll talk about in a later question what fees should be typical on your merchant account and which ones should raise suspicion if they appear on your monthly statement.

But for now just realize that there's much more to consider than just low processing rates. There's monthly fees as well. Also, you should be concerned with your contractual terms as outlined in the story above.

Again, and you're going to hear me say this probably 200 more times throughout this book because I really, really believe it. You NEED to have a GOOD agent who you know, like and trust in order to negotiate the contractual terms of your merchant account. Otherwise, it is so easy for a processor to just flat out rip you off. In my opinion, contracts are never appropriate.

Every single merchant that I agree to work with, is always placed intentionally on a month to month agreement. If ever they're unhappy with the processor they chose to be with, I help them board with another processor that is better suited for them. We'll talk about in detail what a good agent looks like a bit later, but one of his core credentials should be that he's a broker.

He needs to have access to many credit card processing companies. Never should he place you in a contract. If the credit card processing company ever does something dishonest or worthy of you leaving, he should be able to help you cancel your merchant account because you're on a month to month agreement, and pair you with another company.

Also, there's the equipment you are going to use to actually process your customer's credit cards to think about. Don't ever get caught in an equipment lease for credit card processing equipment! This is the biggest scam of the century, and we'll talk about it later, but just realize that if you're stuck in a lease, it is a horrible trap.

So quite a bit to consider besides just a low rate.

### What is the biggest mistake business owners make when negotiating rates?

We talked a little bit about this in the last question, but one of the biggest mistakes that business owners make is assuming that they only pay one flat rate to accept credit cards. This is just not true with merchant accounts. You're either on a "Tiered" pricing structure, or you're on an Interchange-Plus" pricing structure.

The other HUGE mistake merchants make is not allowing an agent to take a look at their monthly processing statement for a side-by-side, apples-to-apples comparison. I have often heard business owners respond to a request by an agent to look at their processing statement with, "Just give me your absolute lowest price, and if you're the lowest I'll consider working with you." Hopefully you are now realizing from the earlier parts of this chapter, why that is a HORRIBLE way to go about the processes. It doesn't take into account, the Agent's credentials, the processor, the pricing structure, or the monthly fees. It's also a sure way to get a super low rate on the front end, and tons of hidden and bogus monthly fees on the back end.

Imagine if this type of approach was used in a doctor or a dentist's office. Thankfully a good dentist doesn't just grab a drill when you go in for a cleaning and start drilling mindlessly in the dark. Rather they strategically take x-rays to see what's causing you pain, and then they can layout and execute a plan of action that will cure your pain. It's the exact same thing for a credit card processing company. Because there are several ways to price a merchant and many risk factors to consider, taking a look at the monthly processing statement is the equivalent of getting an x-ray taken of your business.

Because there is more to consider than just a low rate, this x-ray (monthly processing statement) reveals different types of hidden or made-up monthly fees that your account is potentially infested with. The only way a trusted agent can help you is if he is permitted analyze your monthly statement.

That's where everything is revealed. So by not allowing an agent to analyze your statement, and saying, "Just give me your lowest rate," realize that it is impossible for an agent to accomplish what you are asking them to do. Then you are getting in the way of YOU.

Another big mistake that business owners make is getting into a merchant agreement that they don't understand 100%. If there's confusion whatsoever about the rates you pay or the scheduled monthly fees, then your agent hasn't completed his job and you shouldn't move forward with the deal.

Commit to behave like a business owner and take initiative to ask questions and collaborate with your agent to make sure you are clear on the terms and conditions of your agreement.

If you decide to just go with the flow because it is too confusing, then you are essentially swimming in chummed, shark infested waters. It is just a matter of time before it bites you in the butt! It then becomes very easy for credit card processors and scam artist salesman to take advantage of you by slipping in last minute fees. If they sense your confusion coupled with your readiness to get the deal done, it is common to sneak all types of last minute charges into the agreement without you even being aware of it.

Even though this type of practice disgusts me and I'd love to say that it doesn't happen, unfortunately I take a look at way too many statements that say otherwise. Protect yourselves and always keep an original copy of your merchant agreement.

### How to keep your rates from rising.

Again, you're going to start to see a theme here, but the absolute best way to keep your rates from rising is by having a well-trained, seasoned and honest merchant services agent, that continues after the sale to monitor your account.

We'll talk about agent responsibilities later, but a credible agent should always keep tabs on your account and let you know if your rates are rising. Just as importantly there needs to be some sort of preventative measure if rates do rise.

I'm not going to say that rates are never going to rise with any type of credit card processing company because the cost of doing business goes up. If Visa, MasterCard, Discover, or American Express raises their rates, then the credit card processing company has to raise their rates because their cost just went up to be able to process transactions.

So it's understandable for a credit card processing company to raise their rates and good processors are extremely transparent about rate increases.

You'll notice rate increases many times during the lifetime of your merchant account and that's okay. What you need to have is a way to lower your rates if it starts to become too burdensome. In addition to the wholesale processing costs going up, processors will raise their rates for profit's sake, because they know that not everybody will continue to lower their rates like I am going to show you how to do.

For instance, any business that I agree to take on as a client of mine, is always protected by a "Lifetime Low Price Guarantee" clause that I negotiate into the terms of service of the merchant agreement. I do this for everybody 100% of the time should I decide to work with them.

What exactly is a "Lifetime Low Price Guarantee?" The easiest way to understand it is by comparing it to Walmart's price matching feature. It doesn't matter who Walmart's competitor is or where the product came from. Walmart will always price match the lowest price, no questions asked.

So say your processing rates go up beyond your comfort zone, and you have a merchant services salesman come into your place of business offering you lower pricing than what you currently have. This will happen often as you get three to five calls a day. You would simply fax the lower priced quote into your current merchant service provider, and they would match the price. This feature has no limit as to how many times it can be used and doesn't expire ever.

That's the value of a Lifetime Low Price Guarantee and I suggest that you never enter into a merchant agreement without this valuable feature. If you're unsure if your current merchant account presently has this feature, don't bet on it. These types of features are obtained only through skilled and reputable agents who are in good standing with the companies they represent. If this is a type of feature that you desire it may be time to re-negotiate your merchant account.

Be sure to get in touch with your agent and DEMAND that this feature be added to your existing account. If your agent cannot get the job done, get in touch with me and we can discussed how this can accomplished regardless of your agent's abilities.

One key requirement of a Lifetime Low Price Guarantee is that it has to be in writing! This is so important that I will repeat it again. One key requirement of a Lifetime Low Price Guarantee is that it has to be in writing! You can't just take the credit card processing company's word for it. They can't just say "Oh yeah sure we will match the lowest bid." It has to be physically written in the contractual terms of the agreement. It needs to be on paper, otherwise you can bet that it will not happen.

## Wrapping it up

In this chapter, we've discussed all things with regards to credit card processing rates. While this is not an all-encompassing text on processing rates, you should be much more informed in the shopping process. Now you have a basic understanding of the way rates work, and how to not get taken advantage of if you find yourself in a discussion about rates with a credit card processing salesman.

So don't let yourself be blinded by the rate discussion. There are many other things to consider besides a low rate structure. Put away the rose colored glasses and realize that just because you have managed to negotiate low rates, doesn't mean that your account is not riddled with hidden or made-up monthly fees and crappy contractual terms.

# WAYS YOUR BUSINESS IS MOST
# LIKELY LOSING MONEY

In this chapter, we're going to be reviewing the most common ways that merchant accounts needlessly drain your business of revenue, due to intentionally hidden or undisclosed costs.

Throughout this book I mention the fact that it is a common occurrence to find made up or hidden fees on the back end of a merchant account, to make up for the incredibly low front end rate. When this happens the merchant is lulled into a false sense of belief that they have a better deal than their monthly statement reflects.

Even though this is common, it is even more frequent that there are disclosed and extremely transparent fees that the merchant has never heard of, and doesn't know they can get rid of them. This can be attributed to confusing industry jargon, failure to use a qualified agent, and inattention to detail on the business owner's end.

## How do I discover hidden fees?

The absolute, 100% best way to discover if you have hidden fees, or charges that you were unclear or unaware of when you signed your merchant agreement, is by having an experienced and qualified agent analyze your monthly processing statement that is sent to you in the mail. If you've elected to opt-out of your paper statement being mailed to you every single month in order to save a few bucks, it's big mistake.

That's where they announce things like rate increases. You need to consistently review the fine print at the very bottom of your statements each month. This will take you about 10 seconds per month. Your statement contains your monthly rate and fees, and that's what you're going to hand over to an experienced agent you know, like and trust. They will analyze it to see if you're pricing structure is appropriate for the specific type of business you're in, whether your rates are within an acceptable range, and if there's any type of hidden or made-up monthly fees. It is a snapshot or x-ray of your current merchant account situation.

Analyzing your statements side by side with your original merchant agreement will show you possible discrepancies (if any) of your agreement. Often times the original merchant agreement and the most recent monthly processing statement have no resemblance in pricing and fees whatsoever shockingly!

When you sign your merchant agreement, which is basically the terms of service that you agree to when you enter into a relationship with a credit card processing company, they disclose all the rates and fees on the actual merchant agreement.

But oftentimes, add-on fees or rate increases will be applied after you've signed your agreement. So then, the monthly statement becomes your most important, up-to-date, and accurate document to see what your merchant account is really costing you.

If you didn't get a copy or lost your original merchant agreement call your processor and request a copy to keep on file. Then you find a trustworthy agent to analyze your merchant agreement to your monthly statement that's sent to you in the mail. Sometimes processors have online reporting access as well that you can obtain statements from.

By providing these two valuable resources to an experienced agent, they will be able to give you incredible feedback on your current account, and even better feedback on a suggested course of action if needed.

### What are the most common types of fees I should expect to see on my statement?

Below are a list of standard rates and fees that are acceptable to see on your merchant account. Each has a unique purpose and covers a specific risk factor.

Be skeptical and question charges that don't fit into any

of these categories.

**Application Fee**

A charge to setup the merchant processing account.

**Pin Based Debit Rate (%)**

A charge on the volume of ATM/debit cards run as debit (*with* pin code). Usually equal to or lower than the check card rate.

**Check Card Rate (%)**

A charge on the volume of ATM/debit cards run as credit (*without* pin code). Usually lower than the qualified rate.

**Qualified Rate (%)**

A charge on the volume of regular credit card transactions (Visa, MasterCard, Discover).

**Mid-Qual (Qual+ %)**

A rate charged on top of the Qualified Rate. Normally for rewards cards.

**Non-Qual (Qual+ %)**

A rate charged on top of the Qualified Rate. Normally for keyed transactions (except on MOTO accounts), corporate cards, international cards, and transactions not batched for 24 hours.

**Transaction Fee ($0.XX)**

A flat rate charged per transaction. Typically $0.22 Visa/MasterCard/Discover/Pin Debit

Typically $0.15 American Express (AMEX)  Typically $0.25 EBT (food stamps)

**Statement Fee (Monthly Fee)**

A fee for access to online reporting and monthly paper statement.

**Monthly Minimum/Minimum Discount ($25)**

When the check-card, qualified, mid-qualified, and non-qualified rates together do not match or exceed $25, the difference is charged.

**Cancellation Fee (Typically $550, $375, $300)**

A fee for breaking the contract:

Typically $550 if closed during the first year, $375 if closed during the second year and $300 if closed during any other year

**Card Compromise Assistance Plan ($Monthly Fee)**

A monthly fee providing merchant with up to $100,000 to use towards fines in case of a breach. Usually can opt out if PCI compliant within 2 months.

**PCI Non-Compliance Fee ($Monthly Fee)**

Charged monthly if merchant is not PCI compliant. Can

only be waived in the event that a merchant is PCI compliant.

## PCI Annual Compliance Fee (Typically $85-$150)

Annual fee charged once every year.

## Equipment Warranty ($Monthly Fee)

An optional charge to warranty credit card processing equipment.

## Batch Fee (Per Occurrence Fee)

A charge for sending out a group of transactions to be deposited. Each batch from each machine will incur this fee.

## AVS Fee (Per Occurrence Fee)

Address Verification System: it's a charge to check the street number and/or the zip code with the card-issuing bank. This only comes up with keyed in transactions.

## Voice Authorization (Per Occurrence Fee)

A charge for calling the voice-auth center and getting an approval code.

## Chargeback Fee (Per Occurrence Fee)

A fee for processing a disputed transaction. This dispute is initiated by the cardholder.

**Retrieval Fee (Per Occurrence Fee)**

A fee for a transaction inquiry by cardholder's bank. This inquiry is initiated by the cardholder.

**Wireless Fee (Monthly Fee)**

A per terminal monthly charge to run off a wireless network.

**Gateway Fees (Monthly Fee)**

Fees assessed if you choose to accept cards via Virtual Terminal or on your website.

## Why leasing processing equipment is the biggest scam of the century?

There's nothing more frustrating to me as a Merchant Services Advisor than speaking with business owners who are ecstatic about the plan I lay out for them, only to be stopped dead in their tracks from moving forward because they decided to lease their credit card processing terminal.

Leasing credit card processing equipment is a massive rip-off with only a few exceptions. Credit card processing terminals can be obtained for free from most merchant service providers. 99 times out of 100, getting free equipment for your business to process credit card should be assumed and easily accomplished by your agent.

The only situation in which you should find yourself in a lease is if you're opening multiple locations and need several POS (point of sale) systems that would run into the tens of thousands of dollars to purchase outright. When you are talking POS systems specifically, not every processor hands those out for free like they do with standard processing terminals. So if you don't have the funds on hand to be able to purchase everything outright and you can't get them for free, a lease may regretfully be your only option.

That is usually the only situation in which you'd find yourself entertaining the idea of leasing your processing equipment. Even still the terms of the lease needs to be aggressively negotiated, and you definitely need to seek the advice of an experienced agent before entering into a lease.

One of the reasons to be so cautious about entering into a lease is that they are 100% impossible to get out of without paying major cancellation fees. Sometimes thousands of dollars. I specialize in getting my merchants out of bad contracts as far as a merchant agreement goes, but equipment leases are separate from your merchant agreement and are just impossible to get out of. You can cancel your merchant account but still be making hefty payments on a crappy old and outdated processing terminal years later if you are not careful.

I don't know of anyone who has been able to crack the system and find an effective way to get merchants out of the expensive leases.

A business owner's only solution if stuck in a lease, is to attempt to lower the processing costs by so much, that it absorbs the cost of the lease. Based on earlier discussions I am sure you are realizing why that may not be the best idea however.

So, to sum up this section in one sentence, do not enter into a lease agreement. You can get the same processing equipment you're leasing for free if you look in the right places.

Often times within two, three, or even four months' worth of lease payments, you've typically paid enough to buy that machine outright anyway. So if you can't get it for free, it's definitely worth looking into just purchasing the equipment outright versus leasing.

## Why you need to keep your processing equipment clean at all times.

The first reason as to why you need to make sure your machine is well maintained and cleaned at all times is to be sure that you do not violate the equipment's Warranty feature. Many credit card machines come with an equipment warranty feature. However those tend to expire rather quickly.

In addition to the equipment's manufacturer warranty, you want to make sure that your agent negotiates a warranty from the merchant service provider you are considering switching to. Here is a typical warranty from a merchant service provider that I always obtain for my personal clients. Again, it always needs to be in writing.

**EXAMPLE:** *If your equipment is deemed inappropriate by our helpdesk and is covered under the Equipment Warranty Plan, we will send out a replacement terminal to you. Only a shipping and handling fee will be assessed. Whether the manufacturer's warranty has expired, or you did not obtain the equipment through us or your Account Executive, the Equipment Warranty Plan will allow your equipment to be protected and covered.*

*Warranty options may vary depending on the manufacturer, model and type. The following items are not covered under warranty.*

1. *Flood, fire or other natural disasters.*

2. *Mishandling of equipment.*

3. *Spilled substances.*

4. *Electrical damage (power surges are not protected – use a surge protector)*

5. *Theft*

Notice that the Equipment Warranty Plan DOES NOT cover mishandling of equipment or spilled substances. These are the two most common ways to violate the equipment warranty plan terms and conditions.

Other than violating the warranty terms and conditions and damaging your processing equipment, you actually can get charged higher rates for having a neglected and dirty credit card processing machine. I know that sounds bizarre, but let me explain.

For instance, when you swipe a credit card through your machine, the "Terminal Heads" are the part of the processing terminal that actually reads the magnetic strip on the back of the card.

If your terminal is in a dirty environment like an auto shop, or at a hair salon where there's a lot of grime in the air, you'll notice that it is a common occurrence to have to swipe a card 3 or 4 times in order to get it to read and process. Often times you have to end up manually key entering the card info or swiping it a few times in order to get it to read.

Now if you recall the section when we discussed pricing on a tiered structure, the following scenario will sound familiar.

Let's say you go to swipe a customer's credit card at your checkout desk. You run the card through your machine and it doesn't read the first time. What often happens is that transaction gets downgraded from a qualified (swiped rate) rate into a mid-qualified (rewards card) or even a non-qualified (keyed-in) rate. When your transaction is downgraded it can result in your rate sometimes doubling! All because your equipment is neglected and needs a thorough cleaning.

Most business owners don't realize that the cost of credit card processing goes up when they don't maintain the cleanliness of their terminal. Let it be a red flag moving forward if you notice that your terminal won't read the first time you swipe a cardholder's credit card.

Your chosen agent (if he is worth keeping around) should have a game-plan in order to take care of this. What I meticulously do in order to prevent my client's transactions from being downgraded, is to assign a local equipment technician to each one of my merchants in order to maintain the cleanliness of their terminals on a regular and ongoing basis.

My Technicians visit each merchant's place of business at least quarterly to perform a thorough 12 point wellness check on all of our client's processing terminals. This free service also includes a comprehensive cleaning, and a quick diagnostic test transaction to make sure everything's up to speed and processing correctly with no downgrades.

By regularly performing these important 12 Point Wellness Checkups, my merchants don't get dinged and charged more than they need to in order to process a card. It also takes another important task off of their plate so they don't have to think or worry about it.

This is something you can negotiate in your terms and contractual agreement of your merchant account. Although it is extremely rare to find other agents that are willing to perform the service I just described, you might as well throw it out there and see if anything can be done. Otherwise it will be up to you.

Remember, it is your warranty, and money on the line.

## What is the advantage of accepting debit cards?

If you recall our discussion on pricing, you'll remember that we talked about the tiered pricing structure that is so common. With three tiered pricing you will have a qualified (swiped) rate, a mid-qualified (rewards cards) rate and a non-qualified (keyed-in) rate. Every transaction or card type will fall into one of these categories when a transaction takes place in your business.

But what if there was a 4th tier that was even cheaper than a qualified or swiped rate? As you have probably guessed, there is in-fact a 4th tier that every business should be taking advantage of. This 4th tier is designed specifically to reward the acceptance of debit card transactions.

We have already talked about the different risk factors associated with the acceptance of credit cards. Specifically the HUGE risk card issuing banks take on when they loan money on credit to their cardholders, because of the possibility non re-payment. Because of this risk there are rates and fees in place to take care of the risk factors so all banks don't go out of business overnight.

Debit card acceptance bypasses this type of a risk for banks. Why? Because unlike a credit card transaction, when a cardholder decides to pay with a debit card, the funds come directly from their checking account. There is no loan or credit issued to the cardholder. This means that if there is not enough in the cardholder's checking account, the transaction will decline when using debit. A credit card transaction goes through regardless if the cardholder has the funds in their checking account to pay for the product or service or not. Additionally there is no risk of non-re-payment for banks when paying with debit cards.

Where there's less risk, there's less cost in rates and fees to the business owner. It is incredibly cheaper for the business owner to take a debit card transaction than it is to take a credit card transaction.

There are 2 ways to setup your debit card acceptance structure. You can either equip your credit card terminal with a PIN pad, or you can structure your pricing with a 4$^{th}$ tier checkcard rate.

Most are familiar with how to use a PIN pad. The merchant swipes the cardholder's debit card. The cardholder is then required to enter their unique 4 digit PIN number in order for the transaction to go through. The problem with PIN based debit is, it is very common for cardholders to forget their PIN number. And when they forget, they are required to take out their credit card to pay for the transaction. Which means higher processing rates due to the higher risk factor.

Checkcards can be run as a credit card or as a debit card transaction. One card with two options, depending on how the cardholder wants to run the transaction. The beautiful thing about running a checkcard as a debit card transaction, versus PIN based debit, is that there is no 4 digit PIN required in order for the transaction to be approved. They run the checkcard just like they would a credit card, but they get a low debit card rate because the funds are being withdrawn from the cardholder's checking account.

By setting up a 4$^{th}$ tier for check cards you will get incredible pricing and never have a cardholder switch to credit because they forgot their PIN number. It's more secure, saves TONS of money, and satisfies a certain customer demographic that prefers not to build up their credit card balance. It's a win-win for you, your customer, and the card issuing banks.

Highly encourage your agent to include a 4$^{th}$ tier for checkcard acceptance in order to take advantage of it's massive benefits.

**Why your bank is usually the absolute worst place to get a merchant account from.**

The reason your bank is a horrible place to obtain a merchant account from, is because in most cases the bank has absolutely nothing to do with the actual processing of credit cards. Most merchants naturally assume that their bank handles everything with regards to their merchant account. Most of the time however, banks create referral partnerships with 3$^{rd}$ party merchant service providers. Banks work under the guise of branding their merchant services to look like they do it in-house, but in reality they are just outsourcing to a 3$^{rd}$ party credit card processing company.

The reason this is a problem for you, is because banks are unnecessary middle-men that charge huge rate and fee markups (essentially a referral fee to pay themselves), for outsourcing your merchant account. The bank usually handles your initial paper work, but the service, processing, equipment, and statements come from a 3$^{rd}$ party who usually brands the statements to look like it's coming directly from the bank.

This is HUGE residual income for banks. It also explains why the service is so poor when you call your bank for a merchant service related question. They are far removed from the actual processing and are typically clueless to the intricacies of the profession.

The bottom line is you cut out a lot of unnecessary "middle-man" 3$^{rd}$ party referral fee expenses, and poor customer service by just going direct to the actual Merchant Service Provider through a qualified and experienced agent.

## Besides my processing rates and monthly fees, are there other cost to eliminate it?

Many business owners are surprised when I bring this issue up during a 1 on 1 strategy session. And that is, that the second most expensive cost that is associated with utilizing traditional merchant accounts, is actually the terminal's printer receipt paper. It's true.

99% of merchants don't realize that when they sign up for a merchant account, that they can negotiate a free paper stipulation right into the merchant account agreement's terms and conditions section. Now this is unlikely to be included as a feature to you without an Agent who has been around the block a few times and has good relationships with his processors. The truth is that most agents have no idea themselves that this feature even exists.

However if you manage to get lucky with an experienced agent who has actually heard of this feature, and has the ability and is willing to get it done for you, than you have hit the merchant account jackpot.

I consider this feature so important that it is a mandatory stipulation for every client I take on. Whether they ask for it or not, they will get free receipt paper for as long as I continue to work with them.

I un-originally call it my "Free Paper For Life Program." So when I take on new merchants personally, I take care of the cost of paper 100% for them for life. The way it works is they simply inform us of when they are about two weeks from running out on their paper supply, and a member of our tech team comes out to their business location to deliver a fresh case of terminal paper fitted specifically for their machine. They also make sure the merchant is stocked for the foreseeable future.

This feature benefits the merchant in several ways. They end up saving a ton of money that would have went to Office Depot, Office Max or Amazon on ridiculously marked-up and costly terminal printer paper. Also it is one less thing a busy, tired, and over-worked business owner has to think about.

Plus, haven't you noticed a type of "Murphy's Law" situation when dealing with receipt paper? You will have 100 customers who don't care for a printed receipt, but then you get someone who demands a receipt likes its some sort of sacred document. Sure enough that is when you unexpectedly run out of paper. It's embarrassing as you write down their mailing or email address promising to get it to them. Even if it means personally driving to their home to hand deliver it.

So it is a big relief to know that you're stocked and always have a continuous flow of receipt paper, guaranteed by your agent and merchant service provider. If you are going to take the time to negotiate or renegotiate your merchant account, don't settle for anything less.

## What is PCI, and how is it important?

You may or may not know that all merchants that accept Visa and MasterCard payments are required to become Payment Card Industry (PCI) compliant.

The Payment Card Industry Security Standards Council is comprised of the major credit card associations (Visa, MasterCard, American Express, Discover and JCB), and they have established a set of security standards to ensure that merchants follow best practices in order to reduce credit card fraud and security breaches.

What this actually means to you as a business owner, is that you need to take an online questionnaire (called the SAQ) once per year, in order remain in compliance with the card associations, and to avoid potential liability for your business. By becoming and remaining PCI compliant at all times, you are essentially taking out an insurance policy on your business that protects you against stolen and fraudulent credit card activity that can take place by having a merchant account. PCI compliance is no joke and needs to be taken seriously.

If you are non-compliant this will be reflected on you monthly fees with a penalty fee every month you are non-compliant. So not only are you non-compliant with potential liability, you are paying a monthly fee that gives you no protection whatsoever. I have seen the monthly non-compliance fee be anywhere in the range of $25-$45 per month! This is like paying for an auto insurance policy every month, getting into an accident, and having no coverage.

Usually your Merchant Service Provider has a link to the SAQ and more education on PCI compliance on their websites. When you sign up for an account you can expect this type of language somewhere in your merchant agreement: *It is your responsibility, as a merchant accepting credit and debit card payments, to safeguard customer card data. Merchants must uphold their PCI Compliant status at all times to avoid non-compliance fees and other potential related charges and assessments.*

Unfortunately Agents are prohibited from helping merchants with the SAQ. There are serious penalties in place for agents who violate this requirement. However, the can remind you when your PCI compliance status is coming up for renewal, and get you in touch with your Merchant Service Provider's PCI compliance department. Your Merchant Service Provider can literally walk you through the entire process in a matter of minutes.

If you are not sure if you are PCI compliant, chances are you are not. If you are wondering why you haven't been notified of your non-compliance status, it is because non-compliance monthly fees are serious revenue generators for credit card processing companies.

So they may notify you, by a pathetic attempt to place your non-compliance status in extra small fine print on one of your monthly statements. Or an email from a company you have never heard of (most PCI companies are outsourced) that went right to your spam mail.

You need to be proactive and embrace that it is up to you to become and maintain your PCI compliance.

## How to save your biggest money-making resource - your time.

The biggest way to protect your time against hours on hold with customer service, and tinkering with your malfunctioning credit card terminal, is to have an expert set it up and continually maintain it so you don't have to. As you are already aware, you don't make money when you are required (or require a staff member) to make customer service calls to work on your credit card terminal. Make no mistake, a poorly structured merchant account can eat up hours on end.

Getting setup properly takes a number of factors and abilities into consideration and should not be taken lightly, if you want to be able to spend your time doing things that actually make (not cost) you money. Enlisting a competent agent is first and foremost. Again an experienced and qualified agent is no doubt your greatest asset. After you are setup properly, you need to have regular agent initiated checkups.

They need to keep an eye on your machine to make sure it's always functioning properly so your transactions are not being continually downgraded to higher rates. This will cost you big money without you even knowing it.

Make sure before you sign up with a credit card processing company that you call into their customer service center to see how long their typical wait times are. The best customer service centers have a Call-Back feature. At the beginning of the call, if you are on hold, they allow you to leave your phone number so you don't have to remain on hold. Then they call you back when you are next in line! This is a surprisingly rare feature to most merchant service customer service centers.

You also need to ensure that your agent monitors your transaction activity on the back end on a regular basis. He should be searching for rate increases, and transactions that could cause red-flags with your provider so your funds aren't placed on hold. This can be a nightmare experience that eats up an incredible amount of valuable money making time to straighten out.

By having your account setup properly from the get go your Aspirin bill will be reduced and you will avoid unnecessary rate increases and monthly fees.

### Wrapping it up.

In this chapter I gave you a lot of areas of your merchant account to check up on. Start with looking at your merchant agreement. Make sure you have a copy and hold on to it so you can compare it to your monthly statements. If you don't get them, make a call and request to have them mailed monthly to you.

By doing the things that I suggested in this chapter,

you'll be on the right pricing structure for your business, avoid potential fees and liability, eliminate the cost of receipt paper forever, and have a system that runs on auto-pilot.

# SECRET MONEY SAVING FEATURES TO PUSH FOR

In this chapter I'm going to be shifting the subject from rates and fees to other things that business owners don't typically even think about when negotiating their merchant accounts.

Most of the time, business owners look at all these subjects as individual pieces of a puzzle that have no correlation with one another. But the fact is your Merchant Service Provider should provide you with more than just a good rate and monthly fees.

Let's look at a few of them.

### What equipment can I expect to get for free?

Well, the answer to this depends on the type of business you are in and what your processing requirements entail.

A traditional brick and mortar retail business who usually takes transactions face-to-face is going to require a different credit card terminal to process electronic transactions, versus an online e-commerce store who takes 100% of their transactions though an online gateway that is connected to a shopping cart.

Having said all that, there's not one type of business that I have worked with, that I haven't been able to secure free processing equipment for. Like always, the agent you select to work with will be integral in negotiating free equipment for you. The only exception will be for large chain superstores who require multiple POS (Point of Sale) systems. We talked about this already when we discussed leases. So I will leave this exception at that.

If you're a brick and mortar business who makes the majority its money in its local market, you will no doubt require stand alone, counter-top terminal that you physically use to swipe, insert, or scan credit cards. If your agent has any ability or experience, he will secure this for you for free.

By the way, if you have a merchant account through your local bank, don't ever expect to get free equipment. Because they outsource their merchant services and make it look like they are the ones doing the processing, they are just middle-men. Because they are middle-men, they make it worth their time to refer merchant accounts to a 3$^{rd}$ party processor they have established a relationship with, by charging for things like equipment costs.

The bank is usually charged a wholesale cost by its referral partner processor for the equipment, and are able to pocket anything they charge above that wholesale cost. For example:

A bank makes a relationship with a processor and can offer its business bank members a credit card terminal for $450. That is the wholesale cost for the bank to offer this piece of equipment for its members. But rather than charging $450, it charges $750 to buy the piece of equipment. In this case it would make $350 every time a business opened a merchant account at its bank.

So if you are fortunate enough not to be with your bank, push hard for free equipment. You are sure to get it with a skilled agent. Especially if you're only using one or two terminals to take all the transactions in your business.

You may not be able to get 100% of the cost of equipment covered if you are one of the bigger guys using 10 or 11 types of credit card processing terminals. But your agent might be able to secure wholesale pricing for you versus pricey, marked-up retail cost.

### What if I am not tech savvy and don't feel comfortable setting up a new system all by myself?

If you are not tech savvy and you prefer all things "old school" or even if you are tech savvy, credit card processing is really confusing. That's why you are taking the time to read or skim through this book as a reference.

It's not a common sense subject. If it were easy to understand, there would be no need for trusted agents and rigorous attention to detail when negotiating merchant agreements.

Another frustrating point to consider when obtaining a merchant account through a local bank who outsources, is because they are not the processor, you are expected to figure everything out for yourself. That includes the initial setup and installation of your machine, testing it to make sure the transactions are going through and the funds are depositing to the right account, familiarizing yourself and your staff on how to use the new equipment, and troubleshooting any problems that may arise. Talk about a time slayer.

It can be a very frustrating experience. So, again, if half of the battle is getting it setup correctly from the start, and you take the time to negotiate favorable terms and conditions worked into your merchant agreement, don't do yourself the disservice of trying to install your system yourself.

So then, this is a condition you need to work out with your agent. Often times merchant service providers will offer an over the phone tech support person to walk you through the setup of your terminal. This is better than nothing. Still don't settle. Push for a local expert technician to come out to your business and set it up for you. This is not an unreasonable request by any means.

Business owners go weeks, tinkering with the settings and learning their new system by trial and error. Often times at a cost they would feel sick about if seen on paper.

Not tech savvy? Don't worry. Get an expert technician to do it for you. With no intention of belittling your intelligence, they can accomplish in 15 minutes what it would take you weeks or months to figure out. So enlist their expertise.

## How to get free cleaning to maintain your system?

Like everything else in your merchant agreement, regular cleaning and maintenance of your processing terminal needs to be included before you sign paperwork. Make sure that along with your competitive rates, low fees, free paper and a local technician to set you up, that you also include the cost of free terminal cleaning cards.

Terminal cleaning cards (look them up on Amazon) are special packaged plastic credit cards that are soaked in 100% alcohol. You take the cards out of their alcohol soaked packaging and run them through your machine, like you would any other credit card. When you do this you will notice the card cleaners pick up all sorts of dirt and grime that prevent your machine from functioning properly.

If left uncleaned this dirt and grime will cause your machine to "downgrade" your transactions from a qualified rate, to a mid or non-qualified rate. This will many times double your rates and cost to process cards.

So it is important that it is removed. Additionally it is important that your merchant service provider regularly supply's you will a case of them for free when you need them.

As you have probably caught onto by now, I enjoy the luxury, local, do it for you type of approach for those I work with. That's why all of my personal clients that I agree to work with enjoy a local service technician that comes out to their business on a regular basis, and provides cleaning cards for them when needed. They also clean their machines at no cost to the merchant whatsoever.

For those clients who are in other states, we are sure to mail an adequate supply of cleaning cards on a regular basis for them. We make sure they have plenty in stock for regular maintenance and care of their machine.

Like the free paper program, it is hard to find merchant service providers and agents who are willing to provide this type of service. Regardless you need to push for it. Not only does it save you money by preventing your transactions from being "downgraded" it keeps your equipment warranty valid should you need to replace your terminal. Important stuff here.

### How do I avoid contracts?

Before I tell you how to avoid getting into contracts, let me tell you why you want to avoid getting into contracts.

Credit card processing companies are notorious for their ridiculous contractual terms that they weasel merchants into.

The way it typically works is you're usually on a three to five year standard processing contract. This in part depends on the processing company you use. Within these contracts it states that there are time diminishing cancellation fees for leaving the processing company early. The call it an early termination fee (ETF). For example:

*Let's say you're on a standard three-year contract, and if you leave during the first year of that contract it's $1,100 ETF to get out of it. If you leave during the second year of the contract, it's a $750 ETF to get out. If you leave during the last year of the contract, it's a $500 ETF to get out.*

Although these are actually pretty conservative numbers, I've seen situations where there are seven-year contracts with thousands and thousands of dollars in cancellation fees. This is a horrible situation to find yourself in, and your agent hasn't done his job very well if you find yourself in an agreement like that. So, don't ever sign an agreement like that until you know it is on a month to month arrangement.

I believe contracts are no longer appropriate in credit card processing. If the industry was honest, straightforward, and with a proven track record of doing the right thing, just because it's the right thing to do, than contracts may be appropriate. But that is not the case on a large scale.

Don't settle for anything less than a month to month agreement with no early termination fees. If your agent tries to convince you that a contract is worth entering into, seriously consider the circumstances and all of your options. Maybe even get a second opinion.

This all sounds very simplistic and obvious, but I can't tell you how many businesses I work with daily during my consultations, who have no idea they are locked into a long term contract with huge ETF's.

Advice worth revisiting: Make sure to keep your original merchant agreement on file at all times. Compare it to your monthly statements to make sure you are being charged what you were promised. Never sign it until your agent shows you in writing that you are on a month-to-month agreement with no early termination fees. That's the best way to go about it.

## What if I'm already stuck in a contract?

I am going to give it to you straight here. If you're already stuck in a contract, then you and your agent have a little bit of work ahead of you. The first thing you need to do is figure out what your Early Termination Fee would be, if you canceled your merchant account today. Also check and see how far away you are from that ETF being reduced down due to another year passing by on your merchant agreement.

Next you need to connect with your agent, who NEEDS to be a broker. If he is not a broker, chances are his options will be extremely limited and he might not be able to help you at the end of the day. Obviously provide a copy of your original merchant agreement, along with a copy of your most recent monthly statement for him to analyze.

Next your agent should send a copy of your monthly processing statement out to all of his processing companies. Pretty hard to do this if he is not a broker. The agent should advise all processors that he is shopping your account and that they are in a bidding war against other processors.

The goal is to get the processors to agree to pay either part or for all of your ETF to switch your merchant account over to them. Now, your account can't already have such low pricing, that they lose money by doing this. That doesn't make sense for anybody. Know that merchant service providers want your business really bad. So much so that it has become standard for skilled agents to get them to cover the cost of your cancellation fee to switch processors.

Understand that merchant account shopping is a very negotiable process. That is one reason I love it. Once you get good at it, anything can happen. For agents who survive and thrive, the possibilities are endless. This of course, directly affects business owners who are smart enough to employ the help of a skilled and experienced agent.

Now even if you have a very large early termination fee, you'd be surprised how many times you can get the cost 100% covered. If not 100% go for 75% or 50%. Anything is better than nothing. Of course like everything else we talk about, it needs to be written down in your merchant agreement.

Often times it makes sense to switch even if they only cover half of the ETF cost. You have to factor in the savings you will be receiving by switching processors. If you're saving a couple hundred dollars every 1, 2 or 3 months, than you will pay your ETF off in rate reducing savings quickly. Plus, who wants to continue to do business with a merchant service provider who snaked them into a bogus contract with high cancellation fees in the first place?

The school of thought that I subscribe to believes that everything should be month-to-month, and that a processing company should be required to earn your business month after month in order to keep your business. Not because you're stuck in a contract and can't leave because of a large ETF. Nuts to that!

### How can I avoid the risk of switching merchant accounts?

First off, what is the risk of switch merchant account providers? Usually it entails a merchant service company not holding up their end of the bargain with regards to your pricing. You think you are getting this killer low rate that they promised, only to realize that all of your transactions fell into a tier with a rate twice as high as the one you were fixated on. You try to cancel but realized that you just signed a 3 year agreement with a $1,500 cancellation fee if you cancel within the first year. This is an extremely common scenario I have seen all too often.

So let's start with the question we just answered. Make sure everything's month-to-month so there's no risk of locking yourself into a contract. You need to be able to get out if it turns out that your new account is not all it was cracked up to be. No exceptions on this.

It is also wise to keep your old merchant account that you will be canceling, open for at least 60 days after you switch to your new merchant service provider. This will give you comfort knowing that you can go back to your old provider if you need to, while you make sure everything is running smoothly (as promised contractually) with your new processor. You can verify that your rates are as promised and there's nothing hidden, skewed or surprising.

To do this you will have to pay the monthly fees assigned to your old account regardless of the volume of transactions. Put another way, you won't have any transaction rates or fees to pay because there will be no transactions flowing through your old account. That will all be running through your new account. There will however be a few monthly fees on your old account that you will be responsible for.

Typically it only costs you about $25-$40 per month to maintain your old account. I definitely recommend doing this to safeguard yourself against bait and switch techniques. The last thing I would suggest for risk removal, is to make sure there's some sort of money back guarantee outlined in the actual agreement. For instance, let's say there's a  $250 setup fee to get started with your new processor. This is a pretty common charge. I'm not against account setup fees like I am other type of monthly rates and fees. There's a lot of work associated for the agent at the beginning of his relationship with you. Most of this setup fee goes to your agent for the re-payment of his time, gas and expertise. Don't cheap out on a good agent. Anyway, back to my point.

You can eliminate the risk of losing the $250 if you decide to cancel with a written money back guarantee. Usually it is a 30, 60, or 90-day money back guarantee. You would get the $250 initial investment back no questions asked.

# YOUR SECRET WEAPON: A GOOD AGENT

If it seems like thus far throughout the course of this text, the main or partial solution to most merchant account related headaches is solved by an experienced and qualified agent, then let me reassure you that you are correct. The agent's input, ability and experience cannot be undervalued if you are to accomplish the best possible outcome with regards to your merchant account.

But what are the qualities, credentials, experience and abilities of a truly good merchant services agent? I am going to answer all of this and much more.

### Why do I even need an agent?

A very common question when talking about credit card processing is why do I need an agent at all? Why can't I just go direct to a merchant service provider? To that I would say, why have a real estate agent buy or sell a home for you? Why have an insurance agent handle your auto, home, and life insurance? Why have a CPA do your business taxes instead of just doing in online? The reason we use all of these highly skilled and highly trained professionals, is because they are able to accomplish things for us that we could not do by ourselves without major trial and error at our personal expense.

Credit card processing is extremely complex, and takes years of actively working in its industry to become competent. Just like the professions I mentioned earlier. The thing that separates merchant services from insurance, real estate, and accounting is that it is incredibly unregulated.

For instance, when shopping for auto insurance, you know your insurance agent has to abide by the rules and regulations of the State Insurance Commission. Each state insurance commission regularly and meticulously is scrutinizing and watching each individual agency and agent for violations and unfair practices. The same goes for the government regulated real estate profession. And obviously the all mighty IRS rules with an iron first all CPA standard operating procedures.

There is however no state or federal merchant services commission to regulate and enforce best practices for agents and credit card processing companies. You can think of the card associations (Visa, MasterCard, Discover and AMEX) as it's semi government. In order to utilize their network to process transactions, you need to abide by the rules and regulations that they have set forth. However, at the end of the day, the associations are businesses, not government entities.

Because the industry is one without heavy government regulation and is extremely complex in nature, it has become a breeding ground for manipulative, and dishonest practices. Sometimes the blame is on the new and inexperienced agent who doesn't have a clue as to what an honest merchant account looks like. Sometimes it is on the actual merchant service provider for adding undisclosed or made up fees onto your account without your awareness to it. Either way, serious caution has to be employed when searching for an agent that will serve you well.

## What credential should my agent have?

The typical way that merchants and agents form relationships, is when an agent walks into their place of business unannounced and pitches them a really low rate. The business owner then agrees to look into the agents claim to lower pricing and a business relationship is formed. This approach totally disregards the agent's ability, track record, and honesty. It only focuses on a potentially low price and should now be a red flag scenario in your mind. This is a common start for those who end up getting a raw deal with hidden fees, manipulative rates and long contracts with high early termination fees. In my mind it is like watching a predictable horror movie, when a group of friends decide to split up to look for their missing classmate. One by one they start to get picked off by some dark monster. It is so predictable you can see it coming a mile away.

There are real and specific credentials that you agent should possess as a prerequisite to you agreeing to work with them. Shockingly one of the qualities that's very important in an agent, is how long he has survived this very confusing and competitive industry. While this may seem to you like a pretty low level requirement, it is an actual proven statistic that about 95% of agents who enter the industry, fizzle out within the very first six months of working the job.

The washout rate is so high partly due to the fact that it takes such a long time to learn the the intricacies of the business. Plus it's a 100% commission based based job where it's feast or famine. Also, everybody starts out doing the exact same thing (because they are instructed to do so), going door to door offering a lower rate. Because this approach has been so overdone in almost every sizable city nationwide, the rejection rate is wildly not in the agent's favor. So mentally, it's very hard for new agents to stick it out long enough to learn what they are actually doing.

Because this is so common I would put a requirement of at least five years in the industry as your first mandatory credential for your agent search. Five years usually gives them enough time to really figure out what they're doing. All though this is no guarantee of competency there's usually not a whole lot they haven't seen at that point if they are full time.

The other mandatory credential your agent needs to possess is they need to be a processing broker. By broker I mean they need to have access to more than just one credit card processing company. You don't want to work with anyone who only sells for any one processor exclusively. This can cause an agent to try and force you into a merchant account that really might not be the best fit because of his limited options. Despite common misconception, merchant accounts are not all created equal. And all processors are not created equal. They all have different specialties and niches they work with. Your agent needs to have a good blend of processors that cover a wide range of business types. Usually this means he has access to 10-15 different processing companies and he can really match your business with the best suited processor. Don't settle for an agent who is exclusive to one processor if you want a setup that fits like a glove.

The last credential worth mentioning is he or she needs to have some sort of proven track record in your local area. They need to prove it to you in the form of written testimonials or references that you can actually look into. Their testimonials should include good feedback that applies to the goals you are trying to accomplish from trustworthy business leaders in your local area. Agents who don't have a written track record expressed in testimonials make it tougher for you to trust them.

Whenever I shop for something on Amazon, the deciding factor as to which widget I choose to purchase is whichever one has better reviews. I am sure you do the same thing. Why would you not do it with a credit card processing agent where honesty is paramount? If they don't have testimonials to share with you, ask for references to call. Actually call them.

Don't skip this last credential. Earning good testimonials from influential local business leaders is hard work and says a lot if obtained by an agent.

## How do I know if my agent is good?

There are a few things that you can pick up on early in your relationship with a new agent that will be telling as to your future working with them. They can have all of the credentials that you are looking for in an agent, but at the end of the day if they don't deliver on what they said they can do, then you need to get rid of them and find somebody else who is true to their word.

The very first thing they need to be able to do effectively, is explain everything with absolute clarity so you understand it. They need to make sense of the complicated industry jargon for you in way that clicks. This is not any easy skill for your agent to master. But the good ones take the time to hold your hand through the process. This doesn't mean that your merchant account shopping experience needs to last weeks or months so you are an expert. This is not realistic. You do need to understand the bottom line however. Know how your account is structured. Know how you are charged both by your rates and monthly fees. Know the difference between each of the 4 tiers your transactions will fall into and what the associated rate is for each tier...etc.

On the flip side of that, I have ended relationships with merchants who have nothing else to do but think about and research their merchant account to death. Being thorough is good. But sooner or later, a decision has to be made. Your agent needs to get paid, and if you have thoroughly sought out a qualified agent with time in the industry, a proven track record and has removed the risk of switching processors, employ a little trust and get the thing done.

One feature of a trustworthy agent that is becoming a lost art, is good response times and communication with you. If you consistently have a tough time getting a hold of your agent on the phone and he never responds to an email you send him, it may not be a good working relationship. Maybe he's too busy and you're account doesn't generate enough revenue to make regular correspondence worth his time? Or maybe he doesn't do this full time, but rather for a few extra bucks on the side (very common by the way). Also he could just be a procrastinator. Whatever it is, make sure he maintains regular communication with you both before and after your account is setup.

Your chosen agent should always be willing to be there at your business location in person. Beware of the person who will never actually come out and meet with you face to face. Maybe I am old school this way, but there is so much you can tell by looking someone in the eye when you are speaking with them. Non-verbal traits and behaviors still hold serious weight with me, and they should with you to if you want to stack the odds in your favor. The likelihood of getting scammed over the phone versus face to face is not even comparable. Even if they are unintentionally doing it, there is too many details to miss over the phone.

Plus, if that's the type of service you're getting before they set you up, chances are you may not even be able to get a phone call or email response after they set you up.

So eliminate this new age trend and make sure they're willing to be there in person and look you in the eye.

They obviously need to be effective in getting you the terms and conditions that we have discussed. Otherwise, what good are they? Remember, we use professional agents in any industry because they are effective in getting us what we can't get for ourselves. Use this section as a type of checklist before you start working together. Hold them accountable to that checklist. You can build a bigger, overall checklist based on the things that you read in this book.

It's good to start the relationship by being honest about what you want upfront. I LOVE when I have clients who are extremely specific about what they want from me right from the get go. This makes it easy for your agent to get right to work, and cuts down on time spent back and forth negotiating.

### How does an agent get paid?

An agent gets paid a number of different ways while setting up your account. First of all a portion of the rates and fees you pay monthly to accept cards go to them. This is why they got into the business of credit card processing. It is a residual income business. This is why good agents continue to keep in good contact with you and service your account when needed. They get paid monthly as long as you continue to process with the merchant service provider that they set you up with. This is why it is such a crock when months or years have passed by since the last time you saw your agent. Especially if the last time you saw them was when they initially set you up.

The way it works is part of the rates that you pay to take electronic transactions go to different people involved to make the whole process happen. Part of it goes to Visa, MasterCard, Discover and American Express. Part of it goes to the acquiring and card issuing banks. Part of it goes to the credit card processing company that your agent represents. And part of it goes to your agent.

In addition to the residual income that agents receive, there is usually some sort of setup fee involved. This is how your agent keeps food on the table and pays his bills. The residual income builds very slowly so they count on the setup fees to stay afloat. Usually they have the option to waive the setup fee. When new agents enter the industry they make the mistake of never charging a setup fee to insure the deal goes through. Because of this inability to charge for their work they can't last. Don't let this setup fee be a deterrent when working with a good agent. Really good advisors never (and shouldn't) work for free, and are worth 10 times the small setup fee required to negotiate your account.

This setup fee pays them for their due diligence, time spent shopping processors, collecting and analyzing statements, presenting and educating merchants on the proposals and agreements, setting up your processing equipment and training staff on how to use it. Plus much more besides.

You can expect a setup fee typically to range from $150 all the way to $500. The best agents stamp their work with some sort of money back guarantee. For all of my new clients I put in place a 30 Day Money Back Guarantee. If ever they are dissatisfied with their new system, they get 100% of the setup fee refunded, no questions asked. Your agent should have a program for you that is so good, that the setup fee is negligible.

### What is the biggest mistake people make when selecting an agent?

The number one mistake that business owners make when selecting an agent to work with is just assuming that merchant accounts are "one size fits all" and that all processors and agents are created equal. This could not be further from reality. Consequently they choose not work with a skilled agent that can negotiate a better deal than they could ever imagine and go direct. They notify a few processors that they are shopping to request a few bids. Usually all correspondence is done through phone or email. Never a face to face encounter. The bids sure enough come back and business owners would like to think that they know what they are looking at, but in reality they don't have a clue. It is almost as though the bids are in some sort of foreign language. Maybe not even from this planet! They get frustrated trying to make sense of it, and fixate on one part of the bid that they think matters the most. Usually the "effective rate." Then it comes down to who has the lowest effective rate. That is how their processor is chosen.

By now you should have red flags going off right and left in your head from the above mentioned scenario. This is how probably 90-95% of merchants decide on a processor when they decide to shop their merchant account. Is it any wonder that the rip-off rate is so high? Horribly unintelligent way to go about the process.

We've talked a little bit about pricing already, and how you need to be suspicious of overly competitive pricing. Because often times it boils down to not fully comprehending your pricing, usually you've been pitched one isolated effective rate.

Don't make the same mistakes everyone else is making now that you are aware. Get a crazy good agent to work your prospective processors, and let him secure real life (not to good to be true) competitive pricing for your overall merchant account design.

### How can I measure my agent's success?

Measuring your agent's success will be pretty easy to determine during the actual shopping phase. This is when you are at the beginning phases of discussing a merchant account change. Of course he needs to have the credentials we discussed, be punctual and show up in person so you can look him in the eye.

The very first thing he can do for you is secure a month to month agreement. Because he is a broker he will welcome this month to month status. Just in case he needs to switch you to another processor.

The second (and most obvious) thing that you can measure your agent's success by, is if they get you better pricing than you currently can have for the correct pricing structure that your business should be on. What we're talking about here is pricing that is not too cheap that it's not worth anybody involved transaction processes time to service and set it up properly. So, it can't be too cheap, but the savings need to be real conversely.

There's a good middle ground, a real sweet spot to be in, and the agent should be able to explain where that spot is for you. When you are in that sweet spot it will be worth his time to take care of you. It will save you a measurable amount of money, and it will be a win-win for everybody.

Most agents really kind of drop the ball after you're initially set up. And by drop the ball I mean drop off the face of the planet. They may have earned their setup fee, but if the residual is next to nothing because your rates are so low, don't expect world-class, in-person service.

Having said that, really good agents should keep in appropriate, regular communication with you. They should be there for regular quarterly cleanings to make sure your equipment's in tip top shape. They should be there to deliver paper for you when you need it. They should stop in once in a while and let you know that he's checking up on your account on the back end.

They don't have to be your best friend and in your business constantly, but the last time you heard from them shouldn't be when they initially set you up two years ago.

## Wrapping it up

The attributes I have listed here will give you a good standard to go off of for measuring an agent's success with regards to your experience with them.

Don't underestimate the good pricing, features, and favorable terms and conditions that your agent can secure for your business. Processors don't play games with experienced agents like they do if you go direct. Remember, like the insurance and real estate industries, merchant services is incredibly intricate, with many pot-holes, scams and pit-falls that must be avoided.

If you don't have an experienced agent yet, start searching.

# HOW TO MAKE MONEY WITH YOUR MERCHANT ACCOUNT

In this chapter we will be discussing something that is very uncommon to the merchant services industry. Because it is so uncommon, it is likely that your agent hasn't heard of many of the strategies I will be discussing.

Because of this you will have to paint a very clear picture for them as to what exactly it is that you want them to do so you can make money from your merchant account. So read this chapter very carefully, because you most likely will have to take the lead on this portion of your merchant account setup.

### Is it really possible to make money?

To sum up the answer to this question in one word - Yes. Let's go ahead, and move on to the next question...

Only joking of course.

Also real quick, if you haven't yet read the Introduction, go back and read it now. It tells the challenging story of how this system came to be.

This idea that there is a merchant account that can actually make (not cost) you money, is such a foreign concept to merchants. Most agents (especially new and inexperienced ones) can't fathom the idea of being able to setup a business owner with a system that actually produces money. You talk about an idea that sounds way too good to be true. This one ranks number one on the list.

Whenever anybody thinks about getting a good deal on their merchant account, all they can't think about is rate reduction, rate reduction, and rate reduction. So the idea of actually making money off of a merchant account is sounds ludicrous! Trust me, I get it.

But whether you believe it or not doesn't change reality. It's okay to be skeptical about it, but keep an open mind as I walk you step by step on how to do this.

Keep in mind that a good merchant services agent is going to free up revenue that was formerly tied up in processing costs for your business. This newfound revenue that you will experience will then be invested for a profit into strategic merchant account marketing add-ons that I will talk about momentarily.

So, the idea is being able to first reduce and second eliminate the cost of processing credit cards. Then it will be time to integrate a few strategic prepackaged product add-ons that will actually make you money. There are many merchant account add-ons on the market at the time I'm writing this book.

Many arising that integrate social media, electronic coupon software linked to your processing terminal, and proven gift and loyalty card programs. There are many ways to make money using your credit card processing system that you will discover. But first, we need to talk about eliminating the cost to process cards altogether.

### Where do I start?

The very first thing you need to know when you are starting with the end in mind of making money with your merchant account, is to understand the term "Surcharging."

Surcharging is essentially passing on the costs associated with running a credit card transaction, to the customer or client who is actually paying for your product or service. For example:

*Let's say that you sell a product for $100 and the customer decides to pay with a credit card. The customer is there in person and you will be swiping his card. Because you will be swiping his card face to face in person you will receive a qualified rate of 1.65% plus .10 cents to process the card. So the fee you would pay to take this transaction electronically comes out to $1.75. Surcharging allows you to pass that $1.75 onto* *the customer to cover your cost of the transaction. So instead of paying $100, the customer would pay $101.75 to purchase your product.*

*Know that surcharging is not currently permitted in all states, so it will be your responsibility to check with your own states mandates before employing a surcharging strategy in your business.

One of the biggest objections I hear when educating merchants about surcharging for the very first time, is "I don't want to surcharge my customers because it will come off poorly when I add an additional fee to the total purchase price of my products." This is a legitimate concern, so let' talk about it.

If you re-frame surcharging to not be viewed as a penalty for paying by credit card, you will be able to implement this with no blow-back whatsoever.

Know that there are two groups of customers within your client or customer base that you need to think about when implementing surcharging. Those who pay with cash, and those who pay with credit cards. Those who pay with cash are often "Dave Ramsey" (respect and admire Dave Ramsey by the way) type of people. They're on strict cash budgets and they realize that often times they can get big discounts by paying with cash versus putting something on a credit card.

These types of customers are always on the lookout for ridiculously good deals and they're in your business to negotiate. Which usually means less revenue for you at the end of the day because you are forced to reduce your retail markup on your products. This group of customers are looking for wholesale pricing whenever they can negotiate their way to it.

The other group of customers is your credit card wielding group. They like to pay with credit because it's not a painful experience financially. It's painful psychologically to hand over a big pile of cash that you have worked your butt off for. A pile that quickly starts to dwindle in your hand the moment you decide to purchase something. It is a physical representation of you becoming broke. On the other hand, customers who use credit cards can swipe that thing multiple times per day and not feel any sort of remorse. This is a fact. It is why it is so easy to find yourself in massive credit card debt before you even realize it. No emotion tied to it like cash.

Now you have two groups of people to satisfy here. Your cash customers, and your credit card using customers. When you start surcharging your customers, the best way to frame it is if you call it a "Cash Discount." Because your cash customers aren't accruing credit card fees for you to pay, you don't surcharge them. They in-turn feel like they are getting a bargain for paying with cash. This is their main objective and you have just satisfied it. Your credit card customers will pay the small fee no problem because it is an unemotional and non-painful experience for them if they pay by credit card. Also they have the option to take advantage of the cash discount if they would like.

By re-framing surcharging in this way, you satisfy both groups of customers, and they cover your costs to process cards 100%. Now you're running a system that doesn't cost you anything to process electronic payments.

Now that you have eliminated the cost to process electronic payments, you are ready to start making money with your merchant account. This is where you can really start to get creative.

*Again it is your responsibility to check with your state's mandates on surcharging. Not mine.

### Once I break even on my processing costs, how do I start to make money?

This is where credit card processing can actually be fun. It is hard to imagine merchant accounts actually bringing a little bit of entertainment, right?

Like I said in the previous question, the sooner you can effectively implement a surcharging strategy into your business, the sooner you break even on your cost to process cards. You will no longer be in the negative.

Now is the time to integrate innovative and revenue driving products that are tied to your merchant. The goal of these add-ons is to help make you more money. Because I am not aware of any other agents who can effectively utilize this unique money making merchant account approach, don't expect your agent to have the first clue on how to accomplish this.

However, if you show him how this can be done, as outlined here, he may be able to give you a few options to work with. But don't expect real competency from them when it comes to this. Take it easy on them. This is my own unique strategy that I employ exclusively for my personal clients that I decide to take on, and is by no means common to the industry.

The best add-ons capture information from your clients such as their mailing address, phone numbers and their email address. If you are not a marketer of your product, at first glance capturing their information may not seem like a big deal. But make no mistake this is a transaction between you and them. You can capture information with clever loyalty program that they sign up for. Maybe a free drawing for a Hawaiian cruise if they subscribe to your monthly newsletter. There are loyalty programs that are tied to your merchant account that can do things like this.

You can be very creative with your loyalty programs. The options are endless. But make sure that in order to participate in your loyalty program they are required to provide you with their email address. By capturing their email address you can put into motion, after the initial sale an automated email follow up sequence that will get them to come back for more with flash sales, holiday promos, and closeout sales. The key is to have it 100% automated. They swipe their card, sign up for your loyalty program, and series of automated, and well timed emails go out to them that engages them for repeat visits. Automated follow up is HUGE in marketing. It is so much easier to "up-sale" an existing customer than it is to acquire a brand new customer. The money is in the automated follow up.

There are many products to tie to your merchant account that will automate the entire process so you can set it and forget it. You can also enter your new loyalty program participants into your CRM. If you don't know what a CRM can do, look up Infusionsoft, ActiveCampaign, or MailChimp. Any one of these auto-responders can be constructed to run an automated follow up marketing sequence for 30, 40, 60, or even 360-days and beyond.

There are much better books to read and experts to talk to about automated follow up than me and in this book. That's not the intent of this book. But I would refer you to the master of automated follow up, Dan Kennedy. Dan and his expert team of advisors over at GKIC discuss setting up profitable automated follow up sequences in depth.

Besides loyalty programs there are social media marketing platforms that tie into your merchant account. Gift card programs that can really pay off. And much more. I will not attempt to list the specific products here. By the time this book is finished new add-ons will have arrived and passed on. Technology moves too fast to make some sort of comprehensive list.

Once you are effectively surcharging, and have tied a few easy to implement, revenue driving add-ons to your merchant account, you will actually be making money every time a customer utilizes an add-on. This is a great way to structure your merchant account and it will quite literally make (not cost) you money.

## What if I'm not tech savvy and don't know how to set up a system like this?

No doubt you may be reading this and saying to yourself, "this all looks great on paper, but setting up a system like this seems too confusing and technically advanced for me."

This is a very valid concern that deserves a solid solution from the agent you have selected to work with. Make sure your concern with this is known right upfront before your merchant agreement is signed. Even if you decide not to implement a money making merchant account, at the very least make sure you implement a surcharging strategy that we talked about earlier. Once surcharging effectively you're not losing money. Also remember that customers are willing to spend up to 35% more on average for your products and services on a credit card than they ever would with cash or check.

With the newfound savings you will experience by a rate reduction and implemented surcharging strategy, you will have freed up revenue. With this newfound revenue you can pay a consultant or expert at integrating these types of systems to come out to your business and set it up for you. It's usually a one-time expense in order to do this.

If this is your biggest concern and your agent realizes it,

then he should be the one to come out and set it up for you. This of course should be arranged before the merchant agreement is signed. Because I am the only agent I know of that specializes in constructing merchant accounts that actually make you money, give your agent a break if he can't help out with the money making portion of the setup. This will not be their expertise and they will be way out of their comfort zone. They can however get your new terminal installed properly and show you and your staff how to use the new equipment.

## How do I know if I'm successful?

There are few metrics you'll want to pay attention to in order to determine if you're successfully cash flowing from your merchant account setup. Thanks to your implemented surcharging strategy you should no longer be paying to process credit cards. You've passed on the cost of that to your clients who don't sweat paying the extra processing cost. Make sure that the rate you are passing on to customers reflects the actual cost to process credit cards. This is why I usually advise charging the "Effective Rate" on all transactions, regardless of how it is taken. This makes it easy for your staff and is a pretty accurate baseline to follow. As your business evolves and different revenue sources (online, ecommerce, over the phone, mail order..etc) are furthering your business endeavors this effective rate needs to be re-evaluated from time to time to maintain it's accuracy.

If your surcharging strategy is solid, than any money making system you implement will be gravy on top. Extra cash generated from your merchant account. The result of which will be more money per customer and more customers engaged with automated follow up. Remember, the gold is in the automated follow up. This will drive more repeat visits and purchases, more referrals, and more revenue for your business.

Once you have a few integrated systems in place that are effectively driving more business, scale it and expand it. Or implement some more add-ons to complement your already successful ones.

This will give you a huge edge over your competition, turn your one time buyers into loyal customers, and then into raving fans if implemented correctly.

### What is the fastest and recommended way to implement this?

If you're a business owner who likes to take action, is sick of wildly expensive processing rates and fees, and is ready to implement the things that we have discussed in this book than I may have interest in working with you to get it done. However, I may not if you are not a good fit. If you want me to implement a money making merchant account for your business, see my offer in the back of this book.

If you are hooked on your agent and want him to

implement this strategy for you, first understand that this is most likely not his specialty. So cut them some slack. I would suggest you pass this book along to them, and let them know exactly you want upfront. The concepts will be foreign to them but will intrigue them simultaneously. Most likely they have heard of a few of my concepts before, and probably even know other agents who have implemented a few of my strategies.

Should I agree to work with you personally to implement this, you will receive my entire turnkey, comprehensive system. It contains all the things that we have discussed in this book. All into one all-inclusive money making package.

# A FINAL WORD

Keep this text on your office book shelf for a quick reference for when credit card processing salesman walk into your business and try and pitch you something you don't understand. I bet once you break out this book in-front of them, they will find some reason to get out of your business as quickly as possible

If you do decide to take action on this, just know that your chances of doing everything we've talked about in this book, are very slim without an experienced and competent agent working on your behalf. So let the search begin if you don't have one.

Whether our paths cross in the near future or not, I hope this book has given you the confidence and education you need to stand your ground against those in the industry with little to no experience, and those with the intent to manipulate and scam for monetary gain.

To your prosperity,


Clark Pierson

# GLOSSARY OF INDUSTRY TERMS

It has been said that merchant services lingo can appear to be a foreign language to those who have not put in hours of diligent research and study. I remember when I first entered the profession. It is a lot to take on when in pursuit of understanding full time. When you are a busy, tired and overworked business owner who doesn't have the time or desire to study the industry's intricacies, don't count on accruing and maintaining the language of processing in your head.

The terms are important to know when you are entering a merchant agreement however. For this reason I have included a brief Glossary of Industry Terms. Know that this is not a comprehensive glossary. The industry is always changing and new terms and technology is always being added. However I have carefully selected the most common terms that I believe you will come across in your merchant account shopping experience. Hope this helps.

## ABA Routing Number / Transit Routing Number

A unique nine-digit number, located at the bottom of a check preceding the account number, which directs electronic ACH deposits to the correct bank. ABA numbers are assigned to the financial institution by the American Banking Association

## ACH Automated Clearing House

An electronic method of transferring funds between banks via the Federal Reserve System. ACH is used by most banks physically located in the United States. The merchant's bank must utilize ACH transactions in order to deposit credit card funds to the merchant's checking account.

## Acquiring Bank (Merchant Bank)

A bank that has a business relationship with a merchant receives all credit card transactions from that merchant and settles those transactions. The merchant technically has a merchant account with the acquiring bank, which acquires the merchant's sales slips and credits the tickets' value to the merchant's account. This relationship is in the nature of a credit line.

## Acquiring Processor

The processor provides credit card processing, billing, reporting and settlement and operational services to acquiring and issuing banks. Many financial institutions don't do their own bankcard processing because it's more cost-effective to let the processor invest in the equipment and people and do the job for them.

## Address Verification Service (AVS)

A system built into the authorization process that enables a merchant to verify a United States billing address (street address and/or ZIP code) of a customer to be the same billing address the Issuing bank currently has on file.

## American Express

An organization that both issues Amex cards and acquires Amex transactions, unlike Visa and MasterCard, which are bank associations.

## Authorization

The process of inquiring of the card-issuing back whether a card is valid and that the cardholder has adequate funds available to make a particular purchase. A positive authorization results in an authorization code being generated, and those funds being set aside. The cardholder's available credit limit ("open to buy") is reduced by the authorized amount. A negative authorization results in a "decline". Authorization Code A numerical (or alphanumerical) code sent by the card issuing bank verifying that the sale has been authorized. The authorization may be obtained by voice, software, or terminal transmission. The merchant should include the authorization number on the sales draft to substitute the authorization.

**Average Ticket**

The average size in dollars of a merchant's credit card transactions. This is calculated by dividing the total dollar volume in a particular period by the total number of transactions in the same period.

**Bankcard**

A credit card issued by a bank. Visa and MasterCard are bankcards.

American Express and Discover are not (except that American Express cards may be issued by a bank; most Amex cards other than the Optima card are not credit cards, but the term bankcard still generally excludes Amex cards).

**Batch**

The accumulation of captured and authorized transactions waiting to be settled. Multiple batches may be settled throughout the day.

**Capture**

The process of converting the authorization amount into a billable transaction record within a batch. Transactions cannot be captured unless previously authorized, and authorizations cannot be captured until the goods or services have been shipped or transmitted to the consumer.

**Card Association**

MasterCard International, Visa U.S.A. Inc. card associations are corporate entities that own their respective service marks, administer the issuing, acquiring and processing rules, and set pricing. The associations have banks as members; those member banks have the various powers to issue cards as well as to sponsor ISO/MSP's to acquire merchant accounts.

**Card Verification Value – Visa (CVV 2) / Card Validation Code –MasterCard (CVC 2)**

A three-digit value printed in the signature panel on the back of a MasterCard or Visa card. This value is a security feature designed to crosscheck the information embossed on the card.

**Cardholder**

Any person who opens a credit card account and makes purchases using a credit card.

**Cash Reserve Account Days**

The number of days as indicated in the Merchant Bankcard Services Agreement that funds will be set aside in the Reserve Account.

**Cash Reserve Amount Percentage**

The percentage of settled transactions set aside in the merchant Reserve Account.

## Certification Authority

A secure third-party organization that can verify the identity and origin of a person or component, such as a website. VeriSign is the leading certification authority.

## Chargeback

A credit card transaction that is billed back to the merchant who made the sale. This happens when a credit cardholder disputes a charge on their bill by claiming the product was never delivered or the cardholder was dissatisfied with it in some way. The merchant must respond to the charge back and provide proof that the product or service was provided to the customer. Cardholders are supposed to try to obtain satisfaction from the merchant before disputing the bill with the credit card issuer.

## Chargeback Ratio

The amount of sale transactions divided by the amount of chargebacks received in any given month. This is calculated using either the item count of both or the dollar amount of both.

## Credit Deposit

The value of a merchant's credit card purchases that are credited to its bank account after the acquirer buys the merchant's sales slips. The deposit is credited. It is not funded until the acquirer gets the monetary value from the issuer during settlement.

**Debit Card**

Also called a check card or ATM card, this card allows a merchant to deduct money directly from a customer's bank account. Debit cards issued with a Visa or MasterCard logos are accepted by any merchant that also accepts Visa or MasterCard credit cards.

**Demand Deposit Account (DDA)**

A checking account, which must be linked to a merchant processing account to deposit funds to and debit funds from as needed.

**Digital Certificate**

An authentication that confirms a website is registered to the correct individual(s) through a thorough validation process.

**Discount Rate**

A percentage rate charged by the bank or ISO for processing a merchant's credit card transaction. This rate is usually determined by the type of business and/or how the credit card is processed. Retail based transactions (card present) will always have a lower discount rate than mail, phone, or Internet transactions (card not present). Other factors, such as type of card, can also affect the discount rate.

**Electronic Commerce (E-Commerce) Transaction**

A transaction conducted over the Internet or other

network where a cardholder enters card data and transmits the data. This includes email, electronic order forms, and interactive websites.

## Electronic Data Capture (EDC)

Entering and processing the sales draft by electronic means. In some retail stores, credit card sale authorizations are acquired at the time of the purchase. Sales drafts are captured by sending the sales draft data from the point of sale terminal to be processed at the end of the day. In online payment scenarios, capture is used to denote the electronic deposit of the sales draft with the acquiring bank.

## ETC Type

Electronic Ticket Capture code that identifies the method that a merchant settles transactions.

## Independent Sales Organization (ISO)

Independent sales organizations play a role in many fields. In the credit card industry ISOs act as a third party between the merchant and the acquiring bank. Many businesses are unable to obtain merchant status through an acquiring bank because the bank views them as too large a risk. These businesses use an ISO to obtain merchant status. (ISO is Visa's term for this kind of organization; MasterCard's term is Merchant Services Provider, or MSP. Both terms are used interchangeably).

**Inquiry Fee**

A fee imposed for all card types (MasterCard, Visa, American Express, Diners Club, JCB, etc.) each time an authorization is requested and/or a batch is closed.

**Interchange System**

The exchange of information, transaction data and money among banks. Interchange systems are managed by Visa and MasterCard associations and are very standardized so banks and merchants worldwide can use them.

**Interchange Fee ("Interchange")**

A fee paid by the acquiring bank/merchant bank to the card-issuing bank. The fee compensates the issuer for the time after settlement with the acquiring bank/merchant bank and before it recoups the settlement value from the cardholder. The MasterCard and Visa card associations regulate these fees.

**Card-Issuing Bank ("Issuer")**

The bank that extends credit to customers through bankcard accounts. The bank issues the credit card and receives the cardholder's payment at the end of the billing period. Also called the issuing bank or the cardholder bank.

**Imprint**

A manually performed, physical impression of the credit

card at point of sale to prove the customer's credit card
was present.

**Manual Entry**

Credit Card information entered via computer keyboard
or terminal keypad instead of swiping the card through a
credit card reader terminal.

**MasterCard**

An association of banks that governs the issuing of
MasterCard cards and the acquiring and processing of
MasterCard credit card transactions.

**Merchant**

A business (sole proprietor, partnership, incorporation,
LLC, etc.) that agrees to accept credit cards and debit
cards when properly presented by the customer. A
business is considered a "merchant" once they have
authorization from an acquiring bank, ISO, or other
financial institution to accept credit cards.

**Merchant Account**

A written, commercial bank account established by
contractual agreement between a merchant and a bank.
The agreement contains the respective rights, warranties,
and duties with respect to accepting the bankcard (i.e.
Visa or MasterCard). A merchant must apply for this
account much like applying for a commercial loan.

## MOTO

Refers to Mail Order / Telephone Order sales, where the customer's card is not present at the time of the transaction.

## Monthly Bankcard Volume

The total dollar amount of MasterCard and Visa transactions approved to be processed through a merchant account in any given month.

## Payment Gateway

The transaction-processing vehicle that receives encrypted transactions from the merchant server, authenticates the merchant, decrypts the payment information, and transmits the data to the authorization and settlement networks. Most commonly used in wireless and e-commerce scenarios.

## Processor

A transaction processor, distinct from the bank that processes data from the credit card transactions and then distributes funds from the merchant's bank account. Usually refers to the computer and telecommunications "platform" that electronically manages the processing events.

## Recurring Transaction

A credit card transaction that is periodically charged to the customer's account. (i.e. weekly, monthly, quarterly).

## Reserve Account

Merchant funds maintained at the clearing bank to be utilized for any potential losses generated from a merchant account, such as unpaid chargebacks or other unpaid fees.

## Retrieval Request

A request from the cardholder's bank to supply a copy of the sales draft usually for research of a dispute. A retrieval request can lead to a chargeback.

## Sales Draft

An instrument showing an obligation on the cardholder's part to pay money (i.e. the sale amount), to the card issuer. This is the piece of paper that you sign when making a purchase with your credit card. Sales draft data can be "captured" electronically and sent to be processed over the financial networks.

## Secure Hypertext Transfer Protocol (S-HTTP)

A secure version of HTTP developed by Netscape, which provides general transaction security services over the Web.

## Secure Sockets Layer (SSL)

A public security protocol, also developed by Netscape, which can create a secure link between the Web server and the browser.

**Settlement**

As the sales transaction value moves from the merchant to the acquiring bank (and then to the issuer), each party buys and sells the sales ticket. Settlement is what occurs when the acquiring bank and the issuer exchange data or funds during that process.

**SKU**

Stock keeping unit; a number designating one specific product.

**Swiped Card**

Credit card information that is electronically input by swiping the credit card through a card reader or terminal.

**Terminal**

A hardware device equipped with a magnetic stripe reading device, used for processing card transactions, typically in a retail (face-to-face) environment.

**Ticket**

Another name for the sales slip or its monetary value that results when a credit card purchase is made.

**Transaction**

One example of transaction is the process that takes place when a cardholder makes a purchase with a credit card.

**Transaction Fee**

A per-transaction amount charged by the bank for processing each transaction. This amount is in addition to the discount rate.

**Visa**

An association of banks that governs the issuing of Visa cards and the acquiring and processing of Visa credit card transactions.

**Voice Authorization**

When a merchant calls to obtain credit card authorization rather than using a terminal or credit card software to obtain the authorization electronically. The merchant must, in addition to the voice authorization, submit the credit card information via terminal or software to close out the transaction and transfer the funds to the merchant's bank account.

# ABOUT THE AUTHOR

Clark Pierson is one of the most sought after Merchant Account Advisors in his industry. His NO B.S. approach appeals to busy business owners who need their accounts handled by someone they can trust, and without being jerked around.

He is also the co-creator of **"Merchant Level Sales Nation"** that is designed to properly educate salesman and saleswoman in all things credit card processing.

If you have an interest in utilizing Clark as your business's Merchant Account Agent, you can email him at:

cpierson@mlsnation.com

or go to:

www.mlsnation.com

55958755R00069

Made in the USA
San Bernardino, CA
08 November 2017